W9-AWV-798

nature's
baby animals

BABY ANIMALS
OF THE TROPICAL RAIN FOREST

Carmen Bredeson

Dennis L. Claussen, Ph.D., *Series Science Consultant*
Allan A. De Fina, Ph.D., *Series Literacy Consultant*

Enslow Elementary
an imprint of
Enslow Publishers, Inc.

40 Industrial Road
Box 398
Berkeley Heights, NJ 07922
USA

http://www.enslow.com

CONTENTS

ENDANGERED ANIMAL OF THE RAIN FOREST

WORDS TO KNOW

caterpillar (KA tur pih lur) One time, or stage, of a butterfly's life.

tadpole (TAD pohl) One time, or stage, of a frog's life.

poison (POY zuhn) Something that can hurt or kill a person or animal.

tropical (TRAH pih kuhl) Parts of the world that are warm and wet.

WHERE ARE TROPICAL RAIN FORESTS?

3

■ = TROPICAL RAIN FORESTS

TROPICAL RAIN FORESTS

A lot of rain falls in warm **tropical** rain forests. Trees and plants grow very big. Many kinds of animal families live in rain forests. Baby animals have special ways to stay safe and live in the rain forest.

BABY
CHIMPANZEE

The little chimp holds onto its mother. They swing from branch to branch. Up in the trees,

the chimps are
safe from hunters.
Their long arms
reach for fruit
and leaves to eat.
Hold on tight,
little chimp.

A baby elephant drinks milk from its mother. When it gets bigger, the baby eats leaves, grass, tree bark, and fruit. If there is danger, the baby runs to its mother. It scoots between her big legs to stay safe.

BABY
ASIAN
ELEPHANT

BABY HARPY EAGLE

A harpy eagle chick is white and fluffy. It hatches from an egg in a big nest. The nest is at the top of a tall tree. Both

mother and father take care of the chick. They bring it meat to eat.

Blue morphos are born as hairy little **caterpillars**. Then they turn into big blue butterflies. Their wings are brown on the bottom. When the butterfly folds its wings, it can hide in the brown branches.

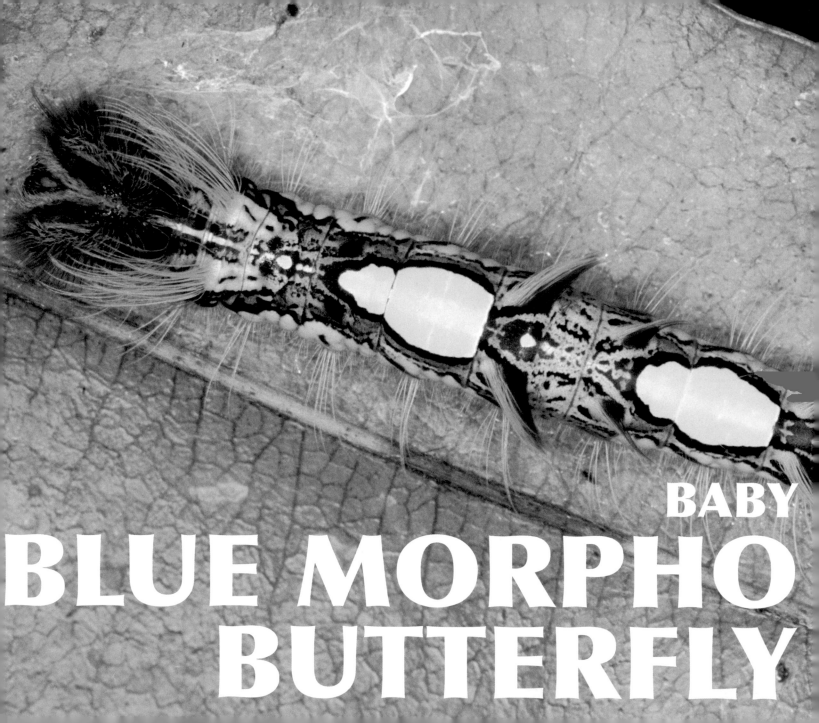

BABY

BLUE MORPHO
BUTTERFLY

Baby jaguars are called cubs.

BABY JAGUAR

Jaguar cubs follow their mother and learn to hunt. Many jaguars live close to lakes or rivers in the rain forest. They are not like most cats. Jaguars like to SWIM! They catch fish to eat.

Frog **tadpoles** hatch from tiny eggs. Tadpoles start their lives in water. Then they turn into little frogs and hop onto land. These frogs have **poison** on their skin. The bright skin color tells other animals to STAY AWAY!

This mother frog carries a tadpole on her back.

BABY
POISON
DART FROG

BABY SLOTH

A sloth spends its life hanging upside down from branches. A baby sloth hooks tiny claws into its mother's fur. They eat and sleep high up in the trees. Sloths move very, very slowly. They hide by looking like part of the tree.

Baby orangutans stay close
to their mothers. They live high
in the trees. There are few
orangutans left in the world.
The forests where they live have
been cut down. Many babies
have been stolen and sold as pets.

ENDANGERED
ANIMAL OF THE
RAIN FOREST

BABY
ORANGUTAN

Learn More

Books

Aloian, Molly and Bobbie Kalman. *A Rainforest Habitat*. New York: Crabtree Publishing, 2006.

Berkes, Marianne. *Over In the Jungle: A Rainforest Rhyme*. Nevada City, Calif.: Dawn Publications, 2007.

Galko, Francine. *Rain Forest Animals*. Chicago: Heinemann Library, 2002.

Williams, Judith. *Saving Endangered Animals with a Scientist*. Berkeley Heights, N.J.: Enslow Publishers, Inc., 2004.

Web Sites

Missouri Botanical Garden: Biomes of the World

www.mbgnet.net

Learn about the animals and plants of the tropical rain forest.

Zoom Rainforest

www.zoomschool.com/subjects/rainforest/

Fun facts, pictures, and puzzles about the rain forest and its animals.

INDEX

~To our little Texans~Andrew, Charlie, and Kate~

Enslow Elementary, an imprint of Enslow Publishers, Inc.
Enslow Elementary® is a registered trademark of Enslow Publishers, Inc.

Copyright © 2009 by Carmen Bredeson

Library of Congress Cataloging-in-Publication Data

Bredeson, Carmen.
  Baby animals of the tropical rain forest / Carmen Bredeson.
    p. cm. — (Nature's baby animals)
  Summary: "Up-close photos and information about baby animals of the tropical rain forest biome"—Provided by publisher.
  Includes bibliographical references and index.
  ISBN-13: 978-0-7660-3004-6
  ISBN-10: 0-7660-3004-0
  1. Rain forest animals—Infancy—Juvenile literature. I. Title.
QL112.B74 2008
591.734—dc22

                                2007029285

Printed in the United States of America

10 9 8 7 6 5 4 3 2 1

Note to Parents and Teachers: The Nature's Baby Animals series supports the National Science Education Standards for K–4 science. The Words to Know section introduces subject-specific vocabulary words, including pronunciation and definitions. Early readers may need help with these new words.

To Our Readers: We have done our best to make sure all Internet addresses in this book were active and appropriate when we went to press. However, the author and the publisher have no control over and assume no liability for the material available on those Internet sites or on other Web sites they may link to. Any comments or suggestions can be sent by e-mail to comments@enslow.com or to the address on the back cover.

Every effort has been made to locate all copyright holders of material used in this book. If any errors or omissions have occurred, corrections will be made in future editions of this book.

♻ Enslow Publishers, Inc., is committed to printing our books on recycled paper. The paper in every book contains 10% to 30% post-consumer waste (PCW). The cover board on the outside of each book contains 100% PCW. Our goal is to do our part to help young people and the environment too!

Photo Credits: © 1999, Artville, LLC, p. 3; George Grall/Getty Images, p. 16; iStockphoto.com © Les Cunliffe, p. 5, Sebastien Cote, p. 12 (left); Minden Pictures: © Anup Shah/npl, pp. 2 (bottom), 6, © Cyril Ruoso/JH Editorial, p. 7, © Frans Lanting, pp. 1, 21, © Michael & Patricia Fogden, pp. 17, 18, 19, © Pete Oxford, p. 8, © SA Team/Foto Natura, pp. 14, 23, © Tui De Roy, p. 11; naturepl.com: © Anup Shah, pp. 9, 20, © Michael D. Kern, p. 12 (right), © Pete Oxford, pp. 2 (top), 10; © Nick Gordon/ardea.com, p. 15; Stuart Wilson/Photo Researchers, Inc., p. 13.

Cover Photo: © Frans Lanting/Minden Pictures